# POETRY now

# *RAGING EMOTIONS*

Edited by

Heather Killingray

First published in Great Britain in 1999 by
*POETRY NOW*
Remus House
Coltsfoot Drive
Woodston
Peterborough
PE2 9JX
Telephone (01733) 898101

All Rights Reserved
*Copyright Contributors 1999*

HB ISBN 0 75430 642 9
SB ISBN 0 75430 643 7

# FOREWORD

Although we are a nation of poets we are accused of not reading poetry, or buying poetry books. After many years of listening to the incessant gripes of poetry publishers, I can only assume that the books they publish, in general, are books that most people do not want to read.

Poetry should not be obscure, introverted, and as cryptic as a crossword puzzle: it is the poet's duty to reach out and embrace the world.

The world owes the poet nothing and we should not be expected to dig and delve into a rambling discourse searching for some inner meaning.

The reason we write poetry (and almost all of us do) is because we want to communicate: an ideal; an idea; or a specific feeling.

Poetry is as essential in communication, as a letter; a radio; a telephone, and the main criteria for selecting the poems in this anthology is very simple: they communicate.

# Contents

| | | |
|---|---|---|
| Noah's Ark | R E Humphrey | 1 |
| Complication | S J Davidson | 2 |
| Cursed | Karina Lickorish | 3 |
| When Ignorance Isn't Bliss | P Edwards | 4 |
| I Don't Do It A Lot | Theresa Hartley | 5 |
| Thoughts Of Thee | J D Winchester | 6 |
| Walking In The Footsteps Of Past Generations | Teresa Farrell | 7 |
| Reported Sightings | Gary Austin | 8 |
| London | Bortolanza Giada | 9 |
| Titanic's Class System | Phoenix Martin | 10 |
| Christmas Past! | June M Bootle | 11 |
| On The Birth Of A Baby | Lilian C Gillard | 12 |
| Welcome Home | Marjorie Hubbuck | 13 |
| Moon Moon | Antonio Mortorelli | 14 |
| My Grandmother | Pam Gibbons | 15 |
| A New Dawning | Rachel M Hanson | 16 |
| The Suit | Linda Laletin | 17 |
| Christmas Day | Caz Fisher | 18 |
| Optimism | Rodger Moir | 19 |
| Mother's Pet | Bill Denson | 20 |
| Love Of Love | William Price | 21 |
| Hello | Catherine Joy Smith | 22 |
| Going Shopping | Roger Brooks | 23 |
| No Angel | Robert Jennings-McCormick | 24 |
| The Ghost Of Christmas Past | Janet Hewitt | 25 |
| Victoria Hall, Hanley (14.2.99) | Marie Barker | 26 |
| Ethics | Mary Miller | 27 |
| Dream Pedlary | Maureen Waldron | 28 |
| Grandfather Clock | A Nicolai | 29 |
| Conflict | Kenn Evans | 30 |
| Mountain Top | Samantha Louise Betts | 31 |
| The Ancient Bard | Lachlan Taylor | 32 |
| The Eleventh Hour | John Wynn | 33 |
| Memories In Steam | Kathleen May Scratchard | 34 |

| | | |
|---|---|---|
| The Willow | Carolyn Long | 35 |
| Angels | Jane E Thompson | 36 |
| The Journey And The View | W Fred Tabaczynski | 37 |
| Classroom Politics | R N Taber | 38 |
| Toty Workerviews | H G Griffiths | 40 |
| Upstairs, Downstairs, Where Is The Ladies' Chamber | John L Wright | 41 |
| Sport? | B C Watts | 42 |
| Our Little Son | Susan Hamil | 43 |
| Despair | Jack Aston | 44 |
| You And Me | E B Holcombe | 45 |
| I'm Gonna | Jan Challis Miller | 46 |
| The Nugget Of Gold | Rob Tuffnell | 48 |
| Spring Bouquet | Philip Allen | 49 |
| Save Our Progeny | Tom Ritchie | 50 |
| Childhood Days | Margaret Eastham | 51 |
| Easter, Time To Pray | Florence Preston | 52 |
| Blind | Joanna Till | 53 |
| Body Of A Black Cat | David A Chamberlain | 54 |
| Injustice For Stephen Lawrence | Kim Montia | 55 |
| From The Gutter To The Stars | Ian Barton | 56 |
| What's The Point? | Don Goodwin | 57 |
| My Love Is Here | Colin Allsop | 58 |
| Life In A Cardboard City | Jack Carver | 59 |
| False God | Jean Paisley | 60 |
| Meeting | G Poole | 61 |
| Sorrow | John Fontaine | 63 |
| Precious Life | J T Mason | 64 |
| Love | Lee Maginnis | 65 |
| Time | Sandra Brisck | 66 |
| Wealth | Jasmine Choudhury | 67 |
| Petals From Heaven | Lois Gold | 68 |
| Collective Eyes | Verna Penn Moll | 69 |
| Wreckage | Jean Nicholls | 70 |
| The Fir Tree | Sheila Burnett | 71 |
| Night Creature | Patricia Crisp | 72 |
| The Life Story | Colin Gentleman | 73 |
| Men | Trisha Moreton | 74 |

| | | |
|---|---|---|
| The Redeemer | B Palfreman | 75 |
| The Flag Is At Half-Mast | H Beare | 76 |
| Known Previously | Richard Clewlow | 77 |
| An Optimistic Philosophy | Reg Morris | 78 |
| The Bishop's Hat | Timothy Alexander | 79 |
| Children | Shirley Burgon | 80 |
| River Days | Lee Round | 82 |
| Stranger In Town | Pattle | 83 |
| Barber Shop Episode | Ann Beard | 84 |
| Untitled | Gail | 85 |
| My Favourite Things | Katie Bill | 86 |
| What A Year | Shaun Gilbertson | 87 |
| Our Christmas In Hell | Cath Johnston | 88 |
| Consumer Boom Bang! | J R Griffiths | 89 |
| The Jelly On The Plate | Hayley Mason | 90 |
| Past Times | V N King | 91 |
| The Eyes | Colin Douglas Growns | 92 |
| Terrors | Brian Marshall | 93 |

## NOAH'S ARK

Candyfloss clouds and lollipop trees
Chocolate smarties and Sesame Street.
Colourful balloons like a rainbow's arc
Giraffes and elephants, a Noah's Ark.

Sand castles, shells and merry-go-rounds
Thunder and lightning, it's noisy sounds.
God's keeping you safe, he'll never forget.
Once you're tucked into bed, there's no need to fret.

*R E Humphrey*

## COMPLICATION

Examine all of my words
that are written of truth.
And when they narrate
its story so meaningful.
May it serve you
throughout the following years.
For a kind heart and empathy
are the tools used for the job.
For as each day that passes by
a quandary is sure to find us.
Which leaves a brood upon our shoulders
wondering which way to go, or decipher it.
Now broach a friend you can rely on
very salient at this stage.
For once a problem is shared,
the dilemma then becomes halved.
Furthermore if they are prepared to open
up their hearts to you with their intricacy.
Then be willing to open yours,
and try to find a disentangle to them together.

**S J Davidson**

## CURSED

She sat upon a marble chair
and sang a song of sorrow.
And as she combed her long black hair
she dreamed of sweet tomorrow.
She looked out the window to the world,
and watched the boundless sea.
She picked a white rose and held it close
but never was she to be free.
Her deep blue eyes were filled with tears,
and in her heart memories she did keep.
For the curse was to stay, awake for eternity
never in her life must she sleep.
But her life had been made infinite,
and boundless as the ocean.
And so all this time she would sit and comb
and not make any other motion.
She looked to the world as the night came on,
and still she could not go to bed.
Never could she dream or lay and snore,
but that night she nodded her head.
Nothing could keep her back then,
nothing refrain her from dreaming.
And she fell on the pillow and let her eyes close,
her eyes no longer were gleaming.
Her hair is hanging in the river,
her lips dry, and white are her clothes.
She is lying on the bank alone in the world,
and on her chest, is a rose.

*Karina Lickorish*

## When Ignorance Isn't Bliss

Other people are a pain
when the words you say go through their heads.
In one ear . . . and out the other.
Switched off from friends or family like an
electrical item.
Which had the power turned off and plug
removed at the point.
As if a mist of boredom or a fog of misconception
exists.
Between you and others.
If anyone tries to listen, they do so on the ice
of restlessness.
Itching for you to shut up
As if you weren't there from the start.
Why even bother to try?
Just save your breath
for everyone's convenience.

*P Edwards*

# I Don't Do It A Lot!

Well, hey guess what!
I don't tend to do it a lot!
So what is it? You may ask.
Is it an exercise? Is it a task?
It's something we don't have to do.
Yet at school I was taught
Rounders, tennis, hockey
Not that I was cocky.
I wasn't, but I didn't like it then
And I don't like it now.
You may ask what, and tell you I ought!
Well it's sport!

*Theresa Hartley*

## THOUGHTS OF THEE

Though from my mind I can erase
All thoughts of thee.
Within this heart of mine
You linger stubbornly.
Try as I might to dowse the fire
Love smoulders for a while
Only to burst into a flame
At the mere mention of your name.
With just one smile
I'm yours again
And thoughts of thee
Come flooding through my mind
And yet again
To reason I am blind
My efforts all in vain
My heart is in control
And not my brain.
I have no choice I must depart
Make a fresh start
And leave all trace of thee behind.

*J D Winchester*

## WALKING IN THE FOOTSTEPS OF PAST GENERATIONS

I've been to Ireland a couple of times
To meet all my relatives who I really didn't know
From things I had heard about them through the grapevine
They were all to me that I dreamed in my own mind.
Meeting first my dear Nanny
From reading her letters that she wrote me
Now meeting her in real life what a real life saviour
What she told me about days gone by
About me Da when he was a little boy.
Walking through the streets of Dublin City
Relating to the song about the girls so pretty
Walking in the footsteps of past generations
What a great sensation.
What is to become of dear Old Dublin City
I must go again soon to fulfil my dream
And to meet all my other relatives that I have never seen
To walk again on its sacred ground
Through its famous parks and to feel the past
running through the town.

*Teresa Farrell*

## Reported Sightings

They came at night with white strait jackets
unaware of the blazing colours
they were sent to dispense with.
Sightings had been reported
complaints made.
A culprit had seemingly made
quite acceptable faces
into multi-coloured masks
of a questioning countenance
unanswered they would dance.
The stars danced too
beckoned even
he accepted
sending his imagination
rocketing skyward into space.
He took himself far too seriously of course
but now he's landed
with the unacceptable face
of poetry.

***Gary Austin***

## LONDON
*(To Enrico, Barbara, Giordana, Giuseppe, Maite, Maria, Massimo, Orietta, Antonella, Marika, Walter, Roberto, Laurent, Angel, Silvietta with love)*

'Summer nineteen ninety eight
The Gulliver's ship
streaked across different cities skies,
picked up wildcats, carrier-pigeons
and old magicians looking for fortune . . .
and it's all about these sailors,
with almost empty suitcases,
that the ship's masters diary
tell its whole story . . .

Mice and twinkly neon sign's London
city of who can't find the words to say . . .
So far from who think us inside a thunder-storm
while she, sometimes, shows the sun too.
It's running fast, this adventure,
as fast as a foreign girl's face,
who's losing oneself in thought
in the free emotions square,
where everything is special, inanimate artists too . . .
Inside, deep in me, this grey room's colour
I left home what, is sure, I'll find again
and is not ending soon, this journey inside myself.
Words, looks, friends and kindness I'll carry with me,
I'll carry with me that life, here, run to . . .
colours never melts, everything, together is Poetry,
is Toyland for who's running away.
Is the come-back way just for who need a lane . . .'

**Bortolanza Giada**

## TITANIC'S CLASS SYSTEM

They've locked us in, they've locked us in
the callous devils have sealed our fate;
some wondered why there were such gates!
May the swine suffer for their sin.

They've locked us in, can't bear the din -
screams for mercy, pleas for half a chance;
don't want to crash some rich toff dance,
just to live, save some of our kin.

They've locked us in, we cannot win!
Guards are running now, dropping their guns -
black eyes reflect our little ones;
as they leave, she removes hat-pin

from her favourite bonnet; tears
drop, mingling with the rising waters.
Patrick can swim like an otter,
but the bars are too strong -it's clear

what my poor weeping wife must do!
I strive to reach her, but am well stuck
amidst crushing crowd which, with luck,
will be my death - they cling like glue!

But, as my son dies, most return
to rest in their cabin, hopeless, resigned
to fate which Titanic assigned
for third-class, may heartless ghouls burn!

*Phoenix Martin*

## CHRISTMAS PAST!

Christmas is finally over at last,
the turkey is eaten, the crackers are gone.
We have at last got rid of the Christmas tree needles.
An abundance of chocolate has put the pounds on!
The carpets have been cleaned, due to grandchildren's visits,
and all the torn up wrapping paper has gone in the bin.
The birds had a feast on the remains of the turkey.
Cannibalism for them doesn't seem a sin!
We both had the flu' for the rest of the week,
so lots of little luxuries went to waste.
Although we tried to finish things up.
Because of the flu' they just had no taste.
But Christmas is always special for us,
Surrounded by our large family.
Why would we want to spend Christmas abroad,
when we've got a warm fire, and a brightly decorated tree!

*June M Bootle*

## ON THE BIRTH OF A BABY

First breath of air, first sight of light
into the world you came that night.
A darling babe so soft and dear
sweet sound of life cried, 'I am here!'
You touched my whole being, my soul, my heart
such captured love will ne'er depart.

The dreams I have for you are pure,
as in my arms you lay secure.
A promise to protect you as life you'll greet,
hope of a kinder world you'll meet.

Sleep now my babe and dream your sweet dream,
may the gently warmth of sunlight on your brow 'ever beam.

*Lilian C Gillard*

## WELCOME HOME

Newbrough had a Welcome Home fund
they all joined in the fun
to make the celebrations a really
happy one.
They had whist drives and raffles
and prizes by the score
and dancing all in full swing
just as it was before.
They also had football matches
played by the old and young.
They made some good collections
and they all enjoyed the fun.
They also had a walking match
seven miles they had to go
to aid the Welcome Home fund
everybody was raring to go.
To know the war was over
just filled our hearts with glee
and to know we'd done our little bit
it made us all feel free.

*Majorie Hubbuck*

## MOON MOON

'You are the best planet in all the world,'
the child said to the moon.
She replied 'I am for sure the best light of the dark night
and all the young lovers love me so much
and I love all of them from the start to the end.'
Then the child asked the moon again
'Moon, moon you are the only one who has a
brilliant light in the dark night?'
The moon replied 'No my child, up in the sky
there are many stars that have some light
but never like my light.'
And the child said 'Dear moon, you are perfect,
no one is better.'
And the moon said 'You can say that!'
But the sun said to the moon 'Why do you lie to the child?
Without me you never can be. It's my reflection that gives
you the light and the nights are bright.'
The moon replied ' I am sorry, I must apologise to the child!
The sun and the moon are the best system in the world
without them we could not exist on this earth.'
And the child was so happy to learn more about the moon
and the sun under the sky of England.

*Antonio Martorelli*

## MY GRANDMOTHER

Against life's ups and downs she stood four-square
waiting for news from San Francisco. There
her husband sailed to help restore that place,
shattered in seconds by a great earthquake.

Shipment secured, she and six children bide,
excited, awaiting new life, new land to stride.
News of her husband's death came one grey morn,
his life from theirs was sadly torn.

After this cruel and unexpected blow
she gathered strength and made a vow
To fight to make her children's life secure,
working to make a home, their hope restore.

How times have changed; when hard luck comes
with loss of work, death, broken homes.
We are protected, cushioned more from strife,
far from Grandmother's grim and daunting life.

*Pam Gibbons*

## A New Dawning

A new dawn
A new era
A new reality
Not recognisable.

To the past eye
Casting over anew
New times
New surprises.

A new path
A new pebbly path
Rock to the shoe
Stubbing to the toe.

Different foundations,
Gritted
Rough
Stony.

Or perhaps smooth?

***Rachel M Hanson***

## THE SUIT

During the ceremony of receiving gifts
a glittering suit was presented to the aunt
of the bride -
It contained hope for the future.
An ending of rifts.
Hand-sewn with love and pride.
It held the lightness of life.
But alas,
the aunt was angry and malevolent.
She shrieked and thrusted the garment away.
Severing the silken threads, which held true
those present.
Seeds of uncertainty began to shoot up
that special day.
The good son of the father
Brother to the bride.
Was a guardian of faith, a messenger of honour.
So he placed into the suit
all the tomorrow's transcribed.
The good son handed back to the aunt
a ragged garment . . .
Prepared for wintertime.

*Linda Laletin*

## CHRISTMAS DAY

20$^{th}$ December.
She's been waiting forever
Now the moment's here
She allows herself to know no fear
At last the end is close
So kiss your cross, the Holy Ghost.

She writes her note on Christmas paper
Waits for life and God to hate her.
Then hangs it on the Christmas tree
And smiles for she will soon be free.
She scrapes her wrists then wipes the knife,
And cries and cries and cries and cries.

They find her soon, not soon enough
In tears, in blood, in God's disgust.
They read the note, what she did say
Was 'Mummy, please bury me on Christmas day.
Mummy, please bury me on Christmas day.'

'Mummy, please bury me on Christmas day.'

*Caz Fisher*

## OPTIMISM

Always looking for the best in people
truth, honesty and beauty are often found.
The very place we least expect it
in souls of people we thought less of.
They bloom in the hour of darkness
when all seemed lost.
And the most optimistic despair
look within yourself.
You'll find it tucked away down there.

There's a piece of heaven in everyone
time after time we die a little.
Hells darkest corner beckons us
when its very fires light the way.
To a path that leads to escape
a chance to escape, to be free
and dance where angels sing.
It's beautiful what honesty
and mere truth alone can bring.

***Rodger Moir***

## MOTHER'S PET

As a child were you ever mother's pet?
Or were you simply told 'Eat ya tea,
it's all you'll get!'

What was your childhood handicap?
Did ya dad suggest a nickname?
As mum and I listened to bedtime stories
me sitting on his lap.

One of mums favourite sayings
'I'll tell ya Dad, just you wait!
No I'm not listening to your pleads
and sorry, you've left it too late!'

My little brother was crafty
made himself centre of attention.
At the dullest party
Yes! He played the clown,
blew up balloons, even threw jelly
and ice-cream.

Couple of times, little brother
wanted me to assist.
He'd say 'Watch me when I wink or nod,
just shout or scream.
Meanwhile it's your job to tidy
up in between.'

*Bill Denson*

## LOVE OF LOVE

I'm in love in the craziest fashion
and with every part of me.
And I am filled with the wildest passion
within the heart of me.
I feel so bright, so full of laughter
so brave and unafraid.
That I care not what may follow after
any vows I've made.
Other loves and other things
have their trials and sorrow.
But my joyous heart more blithely sings
with every glad tomorrow.
Yes! I am wildly, deeply in love.
Though I'm neither a husband nor a wife.
But by all the twinkling stars above
I am madly in love - with life.

***William Price***

## HELLO

Hello!
I'm me
Glad to meet you
Can you see?
The pain
That surrounds me
It's as clear as a bell
The people
Who make me feel it
Can all
Just rot in hell.

*Catherine Joy Smith*

## GOING SHOPPING

How I like going shopping
seeing all the bargains.
Seeing which one to buy
saying this is a good one to buy.

As I have a glint in my eye on the jumper I like.
As I try it on, it seems too small.
As I ask the assistant, have you a larger size?
As she turns around, she says 'This is the last one I've got!'
As I leave the shop - very disappointed.

As I go to another shop to get the same jumper
I come away - very disappointed.

I go home and turn to my catalogue
I find the same jumper and place my order.
The operator says one week or two to receive it
I decide I will pop out to the shops.

Next day comes, the jumper arrives
Turns out it's too small!

So with my friends, I send it back - disappointed.

***Roger Brooks***

## No Angel

I'd like to see a statue . . .
Of miners in full attire.
For the Gateshead Angel
It doesn't light my fire.

A statue will tell the story.
How Lords in all their glory
Watched the miner's sweat
For the coal they had to get.

How girls and little boys
Never played with any toys.
But laboured down below
Risked life 'n' nowt to show.

Working in depths of water
Hewing - in living hell.
Ask - why I chose miners?
Such a story they can tell.

They who built mountains.
'Slag heaps' - all the rage.
Only paid in coppers
When they got a wage.

All sold down the river
As pits they did close.
Where are the miners?
All in sweet repose!

St Bede, knew of angels
He brought religion here.
He spoke of pagan idols
That is what we fear . . .

**Robert Jennings-McCormick**

## THE GHOST OF CHRISTMAS PAST

I'm grateful for a whole year's grace.
Before yet another Christmas to face.
It begins long before winter is near,
the monotony of festive Yuletide cheer.

Shops full of cards, tempting gifts galore,
enticing plebs to spend more and more;
Little mention of Jesus Christ's birthday,
God Incarnate in a humble manger of hay.

Toys are so expensive, but parents try,
often getting deeper in debt to comply.
Dreading each ensuing 'Final Demand' bill;
much too soon the next Season of Goodwill.

How was it for me? I couldn't afford
Christmas, the birthday of my dear Lord.
Not to appear a Scrooge I gave of my best,
Reeling under pressure, of sanity a test.

The constant bombardment of adverts on TV
felt like emotional abuse, angering me.
Relief when holiday and sales ads began;
If I could, hibernation my perfect plan.

I'm exhausted already by The Millennium,
scared of the hysteria, madness to come.
Plastic people, temporary 'plastic' Dome;
with bottle of champers - I'll stay at home.

*Janet Hewitt*

## VICTORIA HALL, HANLEY (14.2.99)

On Sunday 14$^{th}$ February
Everyone inside was happy and merry!

Irish dancing took place
downstairs on the stage.

Youngsters pointed toes
were a joy to behold.

Their beat and music melody
matched their dress and ability.

The super new lifts took us to the 3$^{rd}$ floor
where a group of youngsters were jugglers!

There was fawn pottery,
also China flower pottery!

Accordions and Guitars were on the ground floor
along with food and tickets available for lots more.

But time was up
I thought I was a young pup!

*Marie Barker*

## ETHICS

Island race we are with
Traditions of yesterday
Not Euro way
Dedicated.
We need no domination
Of other nations' ways
Once lost, never regain
On our worldly plain.

*Mary Miller*

## DREAM PEDLARY

If there were dreams to sell,
What would you buy?
Some cost a passing bell;
Some a light sigh.
That shakes from life's fresh crown,
Only a rose leaf down.
If there were dreams to sell,
Merry and sad to tell,
And the crier rang the bell,
What would you buy.

If there were dreams to sell,
And I was there to buy.
The tiny sellers on the breeze,
Would let me talk to old oak trees,
And join stars in the sky.
If I could buy a dream,
And there were dreams to buy,
I'd ride the jade-green dragonfly,
Who's gliding in the summer sky.
Then join the spider in her lair,
Release the fly who's tangled there,
And feel the dew on angels' hair.
If only there were dreams to buy.

*Maureen Waldron*

## GRANDFATHER CLOCK

Time waits for nobody,
respects nobody.
Waiting for tomorrow and what tomorrow brings;
Maturity, passion, love.
Emerald green turns a rusty yellow,
just as the pure Eve
covers herself with
fresh spring fruits.
The cocoon cracks, sending
a grenade of colour into the world
and the hearts of all it touches.

Amidst the vibrant colour
an oak tree stands alone.
Its heart wood alive
like the sounds of spring
that slice through the virgin air.
Pulsating senses stream like tears from the clouds,
and with each passing second
time reaches out its hand to heal
and touch the hearts of all.

The oak tells a story of its own,
the grain gnarls and buckles
like an old man fighting to stay alive.
Each curve is yet another year
another story to be told.
When looking at the clock
you gaze into the past,
and feel the warmth of many years
and the time the hands told then.

*A Nicolai*

## Conflict

When the exploding car descends,
Grievers say goodbye to friends.
Bombs and bullets, without cease,
Have never won a minute's peace.
Cowards and killers, by blinded seeings,
Sully the blood of slaughter'd beings.
Generations of bigots - of imagined blight,
Have never suffered a moment's fright.
The folks who suffered long before,
Never blasted their way to shore.
They were met by a welcoming hand,
For famine had ravished their fatherland.
A means, a chance and a way of life,
Could supersede this carnaged strife.
No-one has suffered more travails,
Than, the noble land of Wales.
But they belong to a higher caste,
And do not dwell on the ills - of past.
And England has endured, without refute,
By Viking, Norman, Saxon and Jute.

*Kenn Evans*

## MOUNTAIN TOP

I am where the storms, and blizzards are,
And I shall never turn back,
Because I have come this far.
Upon my shoulder is a sack,
Full with all my priceless crystals,
And a few old rusty pistols.
I have come here to die,
Because I have been living a lie.
So up on the mountain top I shall stay,
From January to February, then March April May.
But you never know I might just stop,
And jump right off this mountain top.

*Samantha Louise Betts (10)*

## The Ancient Bard

I'm a poet from the ancient school
I stick to rhyming as a rule
I cannot type or use a fax
To modern ways I have been lax.

And for those rondeaus and villanelles
I have never known of them as well
I try to create stories with my verse
Of happenings in the universe.

To paint a picture is my intent
I hope my efforts are not misspent
My works are due to an observant eye
And to depict them is to satisfy.

Although I am ancient in my ways
I like young poets of today
Who are clever and are versatile
I love to read their works awhile.

*Lachlan Taylor*

## THE ELEVENTH HOUR

The swaying poppies on an autumn breeze
Beckon forth the winter freeze
At silence on the Eleventh Hour
Comrades stand as the petals shower.
They gather to recall the horrors of war
And from the past a lesson draw.
A time when Europe's meadows ran with blood
Its streets swept by a crimson flood.
A generation of men in their prime
Sacrificed to a cause sublime.
Trenches, with mud ankle-deep
While on rat-infested bunks they sleep.
Unable to distinguish the living from the dead
Letters sent with anguish and dread.
Eighty years on, the horrors continue to nauseate
Yet, men appear bent on a savage fate -
To maim, slaughter and kill
They drink from the cup of barbarity to its fill.

*John Wynn*

## MEMORIES IN STEAM

The train moves up the valley,
Bringing memories,
Of 'The Railway Children' film,
Location Oakworth,
As well as Haworth village.

Station Road was exciting,
Child stars and film crews,
Actors and local extras,
Chances of stardom,
For Lanky and her sister.

Waving the petticoat flag,
Down by the rail tracks,
The pretty Worth Valley scenes,
Filmed in the sunshine,
For future generations.

But with imagination,
Opportunities,
Exist for other filming,
Producers 'Welcome',
Bring in the cameras.

The locations are varied,
Woodland, green spaces,
Roads through solitary hills,
Nature's changing moods,
Invite creativity.

The power of the steam engine,
Creative power,
United through a story,
To please the children,
To interest the adults.

*Kathleen Mary Scatchard*

## The Willow

Through summer rain, the droopy willow weeps
For fields of gold with diamonds on the path,
Intoxicating sounds from crooners in flight,
When cloaked with unexciting strips of leaves
Placed at the mercy of the weather's mood;
And struggling to survive the concrete war,
And desolation due to loneliness,
Within the field of all the fatherless.
Each orphan may be choked by a grey flaw,
Or starved without a channel for its food.
Fingers unfold and let go of Hope's sleeves,
While tears commingle with the drops of night,
All pain is hidden in the aftermath,
And once resigned, the weary willow sleeps.

*Carolyn Long*

## ANGELS

I will always be with you
If not in spirit, in your heart.
Do not fear me.
While you sit in this lonely room,
I will with all my heart
watch over you.
Don't ever forget me.
You're always on my mind.
I will hold you when you sleep,
I will be there when you eat
and when you are afraid,
I will hold out my wings for you.
And when you feel the need
to move on and let go
Just take one giant step.
I will be there if you fall.

*Jane E Thompson*

## THE JOURNEY AND THE VIEW

The South Downs are a place I know,
That I visited a long time ago;
It has pleasant pastures green,
That need often to be seen.
There are many lambing sheep,
That are frisky and like to leap;
The grass is ever so green
That by the sheep is cropped so keen.
Going north from Hove the land goes up,
And is jewelled by many a buttercup.
The soil is of chalk and very white,
In outcrops showing ever so bright.
Looking south one can see the sea,
Such a sight making one glad to be.
The path is bereft of trees
Just as on the seven seas,
On and on I walked and on
Till the day's journey was won.
From the highest point the land did fall,
And I heard some sheep baa and call;
Looking on the panorama below
Was a vision I will treasure so.
Whenever I am gloomy and a little sad
That memory always makes me glad.

*W Fred Tabaczynski*

## Classroom Politics

*Murmurs in the classroom
smack of revolution*

Stuck in front of a television,
well able to tell fact from
fiction, problem being
where to draw the line between
what we need to see, over
endless cups of tea - and reject
whenever we suspect
our pleasure a shade
unhealthy?

*Murmurs in the classroom
smack of revolution*

Made to sit back and watch
our planet being set upon;
An indifference to Nature
but for a public relations
exercise - put on by fat cats
exploiting media attention,
all the better to disguise
a hidden agenda, of
mass destruction

*Murmurs in the classroom
smack of revolution*

Young voices raised in
anxious discussion;
Disenchanted with politics,
history and religion;
Dare argue for the future, of
next generations; dispute
their elders have a head start
or leaders our best interests
at heart

*Suffer the children, hope
of a millennium*

**R N Taber**

## TOTY WORKERVIEWS

I have read a report on 5 text
About how the Toties are planning
To make *everybody* on benefits go
To be interviewed about working.

You know about unmarried mummies
And people on the rock and roll, you do.
Now people on Disability Benefits
May have to go to a workerview.

A workerview is an interview
Even I may have to attend
If I am not to lose my money
The Toties are the taxpayers' friend!

I believe that everyone who lives on
Any form of benefit, you see
Will be made to attend these workerviews
if they are to continue to get tax money.

I also wonder if the Toties are planning
To make my Day Centre pay the minimum wage
The WTU should be moving soon
Hope it is a normal factory not a cage.

***H G Griffiths***

## Upstairs, Downstairs, Where Is The Ladies' Chamber

A bungalow can be a rather strange place,
I well remember when I was red in face,
My son moved into one one day,
I went with company a visit to pay.
My friend wished to powder her face,
And try as I may - the stairs I could not trace.
Smiles abounded then turned to laughs,
As one stayed downstairs for loo or baths.
Still, the ice was broken for that friend of mine,
Blind she was but all was fine,
She laughed too when we explained,
That in bungalows - I'd not been trained.
She's in heaven now and I bet she's told
Jesus the story about I, so old,
But I think he might allow that one mistake,
And enjoy the joke on this old rake!

*John L Wright*

## SPORT?

They breed and rear the pheasants
With all the greatest care
When time is ripe they let them out
And shoot them in the air.

You mustn't shoot them on the ground
That really isn't done,
'We must do things correct old boy,
Besides where is the fun?'

The vixen and her litter
Are safe within their lair,
When hunting's out of season
They'll not disturb them there.

Then out with dogs and horses,
A drink and off they start,
The biggest pleasure of their day
A live creature torn apart.

How sad and futile are their lives
When all is said and done
To be dolled up in fancy dress
And kill God's creatures just for fun.

*B C Watts*

## OUR LITTLE SON
*(Dedicated to my son Ryan now aged 14 years)*

We looked at you
Our precious one
You were our first born
Our little son
For hours and hours
We'd sit and stare
We couldn't believe it
Your eyes! Your hair!
Your tiny fingers
Your little toes
All the pictures
In which you'd pose
God made us parents
A mum and a dad
We were so young
But both so glad
All the bills
We'd struggle to pay
All the money
We needed each day
We lived on love
It was such fun
For you were our first born
Our little son.

**Susan Hamil**

## DESPAIR

When I was a lad and times were bad
I'd get me laughs from bullyin'.
I'd pick a weedy looking kid,
Then, before he ran away and hid,
I'd threaten him for half a quid
And start me pushin' and pullyin'.

Me fav'rit one was Stinkpot Small
And there was just no doubtin'
Because he wasn't very tall
And that really wasn't his name at all,
I'd kick him round just like a ball
And love his screamin' and shoutin'.

When them as ask can't have,
And them as don't, don't want
How can they give what they ain't got?
When all *they* got was 'Thou Shalt Not'
From parents, teachers, all the lot
Right from their dousin' at the font.

Times don't seem no better now
Nothin' to do, no weekly pay.
When you ain't got the real know-how
To earn your keep by sweat of brow
This world's a rotten place I vow
And who said come here anyway?

*Jack Aston*

## YOU AND ME

I know, I'll never love again
The way that I loved you,
It didn't take me very long
To find your love untrue.

Whatever happened to us,
Because I loved you so,
But then you went so far away
And now, you'll never know.

How much pain you brought me,
And all the dreadful tears,
I dreamed we'd be together,
For many many years.

I didn't want to lose you
But I guess it had to be,
We don't know which one was true,
Loving you or loving me.

*E B Holcombe*

## I'M GONNA

I'm gonna give up being intellectual,
I'm gonna just be fat and ineffectual.
Burn G B Shaw, spurn Evelyn Waugh,
And lapse into the mindless state perpetual.

I'm gonna give up reading poetry books,
I'm gonna concentrate instead on TV cooks.
Watch endless hours of Sky with feet up high
And maybe start to titivate my looks.

I'm gonna sing the latest song all out of key,
Pretend to all the world that I can see,
Leave off my specs, take up sex,
And live it up in places like Torquay.

I'll paint the town, if not red then pink,
Be anybody's after just one drink
Take up the dreaded fag, dance round my bag,
Stay out till three, create a right old stink!

I'll wear cheap scent and lots of see-through things,
White stilettos, stonewashed jeans and rings,
Shriek at jokes and chat up blokes,
And no more dull relationships with strings.

And if I see a bloke I like, I'll trap,
No modest maiden me, just grab the chap!
To get the cheapest thrill, just go in for the kill,
What's the use of tickle without slap!

I'm gonna get myself a husky toy-boy lover,
The kind of guy you couldn't take to mother,
And after nights of passion like it's going out of fashion,
I'm gonna take a fortnight to recover!

I'm gonna get real and get my act together,
Gonna get a bike and dress in kinky leather,
Gonna grab myself a man and ask him if he can
Tantalise my senses with a feather.

I'm gonna paint my nails, swear and bleach my hair.
Wear jangly chains, make everybody stare,
I'll shave my legs as smooth as eggs,
Wear mini-skirts and shorts - I just don't care!

I'm gonna do my thing and let it all flop out,
I'm gonna go downtown and put it all about,
I'm gonna get a life, not be a wife,
There isn't any rule that I won't flout.

I'm gonna spend my dosh and get a hair extension,
I'm gonna . . . forget all this and just stick to convention,
I'm gonna put the frocks back in the box,
It's Monday and I'm off to get me pension!

*Jan Challis Miller*

## THE NUGGET OF GOLD

Billy found a nugget,
A nugget of gold he did,
He found it on a railway track,
Just beside a ditch.
And in that ditch was a monster, a brightly coloured ogre too,
And a witch with a black cat, as well as a talking shoe.
They said to Billy the four of them did
'Put that nugget down. It belonged to one of our ancestors and it cost him just one pound.'
But naughty, silly Billy did not do what was said.
Instead he threw it through his window,
Where it landed on his bed.
Then that night something happened, something creepy did.
Billy was picked up by thin air,
And thrown into the ditch.
He woke up in a second, to see the talking shoe, who looked so unhappy, ogre did too.
Ogre started talking and said
'Bring us back the nugget, otherwise we'll all be dead. I know you wouldn't want that, so come on use your head.'
Straightaway Billy returned it to the talking shoe,
And back to life came the ogre, witch and monster too.
They thanked him very much, for bringing back the gold,
They were that grateful, so they gave him a silver bone,
Where it has sat on his bay window sill,
To remind him of the monsters, whom he never saw again.

*Rob Tuffnell*

## SPRING BOUQUET

Was that book
A load of trash?
Would it be wise
To make it ash?
Did that mistake
Make it lame?
Or was it wise
To call it tame?

*Philip Allen*

## SAVE OUR PROGENY

First a band of ochre - yellow grey,
Then a gold that spreads the wakening sky;
Pink clouds in the ever-increasing day,
While in the hollow - smoke begins to rise.
Out there freezing snow is on the ground,
And right before my eyes her morsel found,
a wren stays where a starling flees the jay,
Winter robin standing on a leafy mound.

Why should we seek to harm these gentle souls!
So serenely placed before our wondering eyes;
The mavis in flight as black as deepest coals,
The mistle speckled half her cousin's size.
Leave them to their world - their habitat!
To teach us how to sanity we might return;
Let us abandon the blasphemy of profit -
Saving our progeny . . . we must try to learn!

*Tom Ritchie*

## CHILDHOOD DAYS

When I am sad and lonely
I think of my childhood days
Days of laughter and fun
My home was a happy home
Filled with love
Mother would be busy baking bread
We had very little money
The war was on and rationing
some days we only had
Bread and jam (home-made of course)
We had no fear of cars
While we played various games
Hopscotch, skipping, whip & top
As darkness fell
The old lamp-lighter came to light the lamps
And then time for bed
The thick black curtains were closed
As we knelt to say our prayers
We prayed for safety and the war to end
And thanked God for our many many friends.

*Margaret Eastham*

## Easter, Time To Pray

The greatest gift we all possess
Is the gift of love from Jesus
How often do we stop and say
'Jesus we thank you for your love today'
Even forgetting to pray
So this Easter weekend
Kneel and say 'amen'.

*Florence Preston*

## BLIND

Outside, you laugh
Inside, I watch the silent tears
Running down your face
Dripping, echoing.

Outside, you're alive, smiling, happy
Inside, you're dead
Buried inside a tortured soul
Buried deep.

Outside, you love
Inside,
You're lost,
Alone, scared.

Outside, you watch everything
Inside, you see nothing
Because inside
You know we're meant to be.

*Joanna Till (13)*

## Body Of A Black Cat

At the side of a country road,
Hawthorn hedge hopping,
Two magpies rowed
About a chance to gorge
On a black cat's body
That lay in the gutter.

I interrupted their racket
As I was about to walk by.
I stopped
And knelt by the body.
With no rigor mortis,
It was warm to the touch.

Blood poured from a once meowing mouth.
Its owl eyes were wide staring
But saw nothing anymore.
Claws were curled out to rip
At a life it had strolled through
Before the car attack.

I stroked its sticking fur
And raised up its paws
As if in a religious ritual.
But there was no Lazarus-like
Return from the dead
For this lost pet.

*David A Chamberlain*

## INJUSTICE FOR STEPHEN LAWRENCE

Let Justice hang her head in shame
Her sword has proven blunt
Her scales were weighted heavily
Against this murder hunt

She has failed the victims
Of this heinous, racist, bloody crime
Whilst her law enforcement officers
Just wasted precious time

Policemen with bad memories
Poor record-keeping too
Displayed reluctance
To investigate a single clue

Corruption or incompetence
Policemen closing ranks
Ensuring racist thugs go free,
Young killers not harmless cranks

*Kim Montia*

## From The Gutter To The Stars

As I lie among the rats
The cardboard boxes
And the disaffected
Surrounded by misery
No money and no hope
I can only dream.

As I crouch in my cardboard city
The world pretends it does not see
It passes by on the other side
And adds to my isolation
My only friend is the night sky
And I can count every star
I can see each constellation
And trace a map of the sky.

I bow my head and start to pray
That I could live among the stars forever
If I could burst through
The celestial doors
I wouldn't ask for anything more.

Before I sleep I look to the light
And my outlook seems to change
I forget all earthly things
And touch a higher plane
My soul starts to fly
And becomes a point of light
In this light I travel so far
And it raises me up
From the gutter to the stars.

**Ian Barton**

## What's the Point?

What's the point of being the PM
If you can't hide behind other men
What's the point of being an MP
If jobs you don't get three
What's the point of being a councillor
If you don't get your foot inside the door
What's the point of sucking up to the boss
If you don't then get to buy at cost
What's the point of being on the board
If you haven't got a secret hoard
What's the point of getting divorced
If you spend half your life in court
What's the point of life itself
When half a dozen have got all the wealth?

*Don Goodwin*

## My Love Is Here

Stormy winds and endless rain
Never more to feel your love again
I sit alone and shed a tear
For I know death is so near
Here I sit so heavy-hearted
For very soon we will be parted
All I can do is gently cry
For I know soon I will die.

They don't give me any choice
Soon no more to hear your voice
My sadness I cannot hide
Taken from your lovely side
Pain breaks in my heart
For very soon we two must part
Never again to hear that sound
Of friendship and love I have found.

No hell below or heaven above
Taken from the ones I love
I shall be away forever
Never more our talks together
Please don't feel sad for me
For at your side I will always be
I know that death is wrong
Here with my friends is where I belong.

*Colin Allsop*

## LIFE IN A CARDBOARD CITY

Unlike some fairytale of old
The streets of London are not paved with gold,
For those who live in a cardboard city
The mean streets are devoid of pity,
City gents in bowler hats
Do not see them who dwell in cardboard flats,
There's none so blind that they cannot see
The forest for the damned old trees,
What's wrong with this country, does nobody care
When streets of houses stand empty and bare,
Politicians shake heads and say it's a sin
But still the dwellers scrounge about in waste bins,
Under dark, damp, dismal bridges they huddle
Trying to keep warm away from the rainy puddle,
In doorways and underground tunnels they lay
Waiting to see the light of day,
Begging for money, begging for a job, begging for a life
Away from the cardboard city and eternal strife,
Where will it end, nobody knows
Must they suffer life's bitter blows,
Unlike some fairytale of old
The streets of London are not paved with gold.

*Jack Carver*

## FALSE GOD

First magic of the moment well it was for
the young girl,
the ecstasy of the real thing sent her
into a whirl.

She never even asked him what he had done
before,
until the day he let her see the photograph
from the drawer, she had thought that she
was the girl he did adore.

Astonished at the likeness it could have been
her face,
she realized he was looking for this image
to embrace.

For her he had been number one the ace from
out the pack,
but, he was just remembering the girl who
won't come back.

Now life for her was tragedy knowing that
second best,
was worse than being single now they both
would fail life's test.

Adoration for a man had really been her
sin,
put not your faith in man alone then your
life can begin.

*Jean Paisley*

## MEETING

With what surprise
The rain wet rose
Saw the magnolia
Waiting there
In the summer air.

With singing joy
She turned to greet
Lovely magnolia
Waiting there
In the summer air.

But petals fell
Like waxen tears
From the magnolia
Dying there
In the summer air.

*G Poole*

## Sorrow

In sorrow there is no hiding
when tears have stilled
and emptiness had laid waste
the emotions' responses
and time is of no consequence
there is nowhere to go
a desert of feeling
hangs with the weight of remembering
of shared joys and sorrows
of reproaches and actions
that should not and could not have happened
or did they?

When tears have stilled
hollowed out bereft of consequence
to seek reason for pain
loneliness in a teaming bustling world
where no colour breaks through
the shroud of timeless loss
and then we remember
clinging to shared laughter
when at one with each other
now was important and tomorrow
was rich in promise and what was to become
and harsh words had no meaning

And then comes another night
and the darkness and solitude
not lessened by contact with others
sleep and waking are as one
in fearful reproach
and so it passes as things
and the morrow wakens the soul to another day
the sorrow is lessened by degrees
and replaced by anger at we know not what

the anger
awakening buried depth of soul
and the promise of feeling once again
again we share
for in sorrow there is no hiding

***John Fontaine***

## Precious Life

Come and I will show you the world; We are free to travel and wander where we please.
Free to follow our lifetime dreams and journey through time.
Come and let me show you the wonders of the world; where life is good and trouble-free.
For I know our world is safe where children are born into a world of strength.
A world of wondrous joy; They wander where they please.
Free to follow their lifetime dreams thousands of beings so tiny alone.
A world of muted sound and half-heard voices where all may tenderly embrace.
So much our floating dreams' time has come. Life the new life gently to the light.
To the sun. To the sky; Hold the precious burden; Life the young one high.
Lift the newborn gently handle them with care. Hold the precious baby and let him breathe the air.

*J T Mason*

## LOVE

Love,
Love,
Gentle,
As a dove,
So pure,
So true,
Let Your love,
Be seen,
In all I do,
Help me,
Love others,
Just like You,
Rest,
And peace,
Beyond belief,
Gentle,
Caring,
Burden bearing,
Love of Jesus,
See me through,
Till Jesus,
I see You.

***Lee Maginnis***

## TIME

Within the silence of the room ticks a grandfather clock, it notes every second until its pendulum stops. Seconds become all minutes become all times we can't hold. They each become a memory when another of them is known. When time seemed to pass quickly on those good days, but then very slowly on those very sad ones, there was somewhere watching a watch or a clock that was in position observing our lots. But time in itself has no need of a clock, it weaves all around us and never once stops. It stays the same age, not one care for all us. It ages our everything with its mysterious touch.

*Sandra Brisck*

## WEALTH

We think of what we haven't got
Or what we wish to have bought
When really we are caught
In the world of fraud.

Others think of what they own
No superiority in their tone
But some see and moan
And others steal so much as a bone.

When will we be free
Of all the torment of more
How quickly we experience bore
Even though it's been said before
We will never feel remorse.

But the most contented
Are those who are at peace
With what they have seen and got
When others will be wrapped in the circle of greed
Such a deed should not breed.

*Jasmine Choudhury*

## PETALS FROM HEAVEN

A flower so rare, more
stunning than a rose.
I surveyed it affectionately
enthralled, engrossed.
Bewitched by all its beauty,
envy filled mine eyes.
As sunshine pervaded through
cloudy dismal skies,
It captured all the glory, it
reigned supreme.
Almost lost and hidden among
bracken evergreen
The colour white and startling
blue, no species will you find
So fragile, yet hardy surviving
snow and ice combined.
In blustery conditions it
defiantly endures.
I kneel and pray before it
a lovely 'Lady of Lourdes'

**Lois Gold**

## COLLECTIVE EYES

I looked into eyes
That shed no tear;
I found a crushed heart
In deep despair.

I looked into eyes
Wrongly condemned;
I found faith long gone
And not one friend.

I looked into eyes
Of ageing old;
I found a groping
For human soul.

I looked into eyes:
Battered, bloody wells;
I saw people-shields
For cowardly shells.

I looked into eyes
Of abused youth;
I found brave truth
Defeating the brute.

I looked into eyes
Of starvation's daze;
I found scales wanting
In our moral maze.

I looked into eyes
Of those who dare;
I saw hope battling
For love and cheer.

**Verna Penn Moll**

## WRECKAGE

Boats tied to the harbour wall
the sea is lashing like a waterfall,
The wind is blowing the waves are high
raising the water to touch the sky.
Gulls are screeching overhead
the sea is showing the fish's head.
A boat in the distance losing a sail
a sound, a noise, a far-off wail.
Lifeboat, sirens, boats hitting wall
people huddling, an echoing call.
Waves are tossing high and low
the light shining on the water,
shows an eerie glow.
A boat is heading for the shore
broken up, no use anymore.
Crowds running, coping in fierce gale,
the sea has destroyed, made to fail.

*Jean Nicholls*

## THE FIR TREE

I look into the past
And see a Christmas tree
Standing upright in our garden,
Spiny, green for all to see.

I watch the fir tree flourish,
Heedless of the snow
And the spade that strikes at Advent,
Lifting it to make a show.

I see the ornamental pot
That hosts the Christmas tree
Draped in tinsel, filled with earth
As soft as soft could be.

I watch the tree in firelight
Cast shadows round the room,
Branches decked with silver bells
Relieving winter's gloom.

So many times I've played this scene
And still it brings a glow,
Perhaps because the tree survived
Those onslaughts, long ago.

Not just survived - it seems it thrived!
But one thing puzzles me;
Did the tree outgrow our living room,
Or we outgrow the tree?

**Sheila Burnett**

## Night Creature

In the darkest of night
He prowls around,
Walking stealthily, without a sound.
His ears alert,
He crouches low,
If danger is near, he would know.
The alleys of his neighbourhood
He knows them very well,
His shadow in the lamplight
Casts an eerie spell.
As he stands in the moonlight
So dark and serene,
This mystical cat
You may well have seen.

*Patricia Crisp*

## THE LIFE STORY

I'll tell you a little tale, fiction and fable
I won't promise that it will be interesting, and it may not be particularly compelling.
It may not make you laugh,
It may not make you cry,
I won't promise that it will be full of fun, or sun, or anything bright.
It may not bring joy or elation, it may not bring sadness or desolation.

But when I've sat you down and told you the tale, be thankful I shared it with you, it's the story of my life, and it's all I have. I care about you so much that I have shared all I have.
But now I have shared the tale and we can look back, and laugh or cry or do anything that we desire.
So all that's left to say - looking down from the sky:
I loved you enough to share the tale and now I'm saying goodbye.

*Colin Gentleman*

## MEN

Who needs them?
That's what most women would say.
Bullying, bossy, very chauvinist too.
How many women
Can remember them saying
'I love you'?

Football on telly
Then they listen to nowt.
Beer can in hand, shouting too.
What do we see in men?
If only we knew.

Match is finished
Their team has won.
Now he thinks, we're going to bed
As he says, 'to have some fun'.

He must be joking
That's what I say.
He may realise, I'm a woman
Who's got feelings, one day.

***Trisha Moreton***

## THE REDEEMER

If, in the shallowness of our minds
We do not acknowledge His being.
If, in the greatness of our ignorance
We deny His overwhelming Love, then,
in all honesty, we are dead.
We are dead
If we cannot celebrate His birth
in sober fashion.
Giving thankful prayers and praise
to one who lights our way.
For truly, without Him we are lost.
We are lost
If we cannot call Him
Father, Son and Holy Ghost.
But, if you can and do
then let me not hear you boast.
For I shall think it all pretence.
I shall think it all pretence
when leaving from your church
You deny the beggar, the drunkard
and the whore.
Believing that He loves you more.

***B Palfreman***

## The Flag Is At Half-Mast

The flag is at half-mast today
Our Lord Jesus Christ has been slain
He alone knew why He hung on the tree
To suffer such terrible pain
To follow His ways, is what He asks
To love our neighbour will lighten His task
Day's dawning is a daily gift
Accepted by us as our right
He watches over us day by day
He helps us to get through the night
We need to take stock of our lives
As they pass from day to day
To thank God for His goodness
And the price He was willing to pay
The flag is at half-mast
Today Good Friday.

*H Beare*

## Known Previously

love what is love
the girls often asked
the teacher told them
silence or you're the
ones for me to blame
then all went silent
in ways not known
not ever known previously
all was so silent
on reflecting back it
was almost so motionless
love they asked about
so young they were
they wanted to know
all about love and
that was the secret
out of the ways
of the hidden things
love they so needed
love they so wanted
to them it was strange
so strange yet easy
for them to have
to live with it
that was their duty
the path they trod
over all other paths
so many negative things
the old bad strangeness
was always so strange

**Richard Clewlow**

## AN OPTIMISTIC PHILOSOPHY

As we go through life just day by day some things make little sense
And as we get a little older we find we're sitting on the fence
We see those all around us with policies that make things worse
For they're juggling with finances from an ever-dwindling purse
The problem greed has been with us through the ages
It only varies from cave days to present times with progress in
different stages
For then it was neighbours' animals or perhaps chickens that were
sought after
But now it seems that nothing's barred which does not bring much
laughter
There are many people round us who think the world owes them
a living
And there's no way that they will ever feel the joy there is in giving
With some it seems achievement's gained by more or less destroying
So what chance is peace to have when with the dream we're only toying
The world would be a lovely place if we could only help each other
If we were only content with what we've got and not envious of our
brother
It seems the problems that we have can somehow be disputed
When there are ample resources in the world and wealth if fairly
distributed
We're all introduced into this world with no such thing as status
Yet many are really so concerned with just how others rate us
Acceptance in society needs time, patience and finesse
For it must be part of you and not what you possess
To ask everyone to live this way is asking for a dream
We can only hope that maybe more will fit into the scheme
So should you win a fortune and it seems natural to shout
Consider it won't bring health and happiness and that's what life's
about

*Reg Morris*

## THE BISHOP'S HAT

A hopeless, hapless, hamstrung hiker
Met the bungling, bingeing, bearded biker,
The former wasn't much of a fighter,
But I think the biker mitre.

*Timothy Alexander*

## CHILDREN

Children's laughter, children's tears,
Children's wonder, children's fears.
This child brings joy
As each year passes.
Precious daughter,
Precious son,
A new-found wonder has begun -
For the parents, a longed for child.
Jesus was a child like this
Born to Mary, Joseph too.
They both shared joys and pain like us
But so much harder as they knew
Their precious Son belonged to all.
he came from God to die for us,
Our sin and sickness to redeem,
For eternity He came.
Jesus you will understand
You were once a child like us,
You see the laughter and the tears,
Dear Lord we thank you for your love
For every child you give to us.
Give us grateful hearts Lord
To love as you love us.
Open now our eyes Lord, to see the world you made.
May we hear your words Lord
And tell others of your love.
As you bless us Lord, may we become a blessing,
May we have your heart Lord
To see the suffering in this world.
Show us how to understand
And listen to their pain -
We long to live for you Lord
And spread your love and peace.
You gave us more than we deserve -
How can we praise you best?

You gave your everything for us
You died to save us all.
Show us how to live Lord,
And love as you love us.

***Shirley Burgon***

## River Days

As I swung out,
From the riverbank.

The breeze swept past
My face,
On my river days
The teenage point,
In the river of life.

The time when I had
My own paradise.

Lost in dreams of you
As the sun sets over,
The old river bridge
My river days soon
Must pass.

But the memories
Will never fade.

River days.

**Lee Round**

## STRANGER IN TOWN...

On a lovely, sunny morning,
What a lot of friends I've met,
When my hair is looking lank,
And I'm off to have it set.
But much later, when emerging,
With my crowning glory bright,
Not a compliment forthcoming,
Not a soul I know in sight!

*Pattle*

## BARBER SHOP EPISODE

Well my hair is my pride and joy,
Which no adult seems to comprehend.
Doesn't matter what I say or do,
It's all got to come off in the end!
Anyone would think it was their hair,
Why can't they leave it where it belongs?
I'm marched off to the barber shop,
Screaming and shouting my merry songs!

Perched on a make-shift seat aboard,
On top of the arms of the chair.
I see the glee in the barber's eyes,
As I return a gaze of despair.
Gown wrapped round fastened tight,
Then a towel shaved in at the neck.
All off all over like a hedgehog,
Honestly he doesn't care a heck!

Watching my reflection in the mirror
And the expression on his face,
The clippers buzzing confoundedly
As hair flies all over the place.
Ears pulled to get the awkward bits,
Head shoved this way and that, heck!
I move, catch a glimpse of the scissors
As he takes a chunk out of my neck.

With a river of blood trickling down,
Oops! Onto that lovely white towel
Now he's blamed me for the mess
An adult's priggishness, wow!
So the guy thinks he's finished, thanks
A plaster to hide the hole in my head.
Then has the audacity to charge for it,
Well I guess there's no more to be said!

*Ann Beard*

## Untitled

I walked into a hall of mirrors,
And saw two very different reflections,
The first distorted, misshapen and ugly,
The second beautiful, without blemish, perfect

I saw the mirrors had labels,
The first marked 'my image'
The second - 'God's image'.

*Gail*

## MY FAVOURITE THINGS - TRAVELLING

T ravelling to different places.
R ussia where the wild bears roam.
A eroplanes, travelling the world.
V ans, taking you.
E lephants in Africa.
L ong journeys.
L ots of exciting scenery as I go.
I ndian culture all around.
N orth pole's cold weather freezing me to the bone.
G reen trees surround me everywhere I go.

*Katie Bill*

## WHAT A YEAR

1998 what a year it's been, disasters all around the world,
and Sinatra left the scene.

And Clinton had his moments, some good, some not so clever,
what he did with that Lewinsky lass, again I bet he'll never.

Then there's Northern Ireland, when will the fighting stop,
when will the IRA, at last their weapons drop,
soon I bet now Mo's on the job, she will make them tow the line,
then once again that emerald isle can shine.

And then there is old Sadam, he's at it once again,
we should wipe him off the planet, the bloke is quite insane.

But we had some fun along the way, as the year has ticked on by,
our performance in the World Cup, and watching Richard Branson,
try to fly, and then there was the sad times, the things that made us cry,
we bid farewell to Sonny Bono, and Dermot Morgan (Father Ted),
some of the days in '98 I wish I'd stayed in bed.

Yes, lots and lots has happened in 1998, one more year is over,
we're a year older mate, so have a happy '99,
and pray the year is fine, and I hope that your every wish comes true,
in 1999 . . .

*Shaun Gilbertson*

## OUR CHRISTMAS IN HELL

Children screaming, nowhere to hide
Noisy neighbours on the other side
They're drinking, shouting, drugs and beer
They shouted 'Does Jesus want a good cheer?'
Is this what Christmas is all about?
'Bible bashers,' they would shout
'Do we have to live here God?' I cried
'Pray like mad,' I heard him reply
We had this every day and night, gangs
Three and four gangs, a gun, and bang
I thought at the time this is like hell
Then I remembered my friend Jesus I can tell.
We put up with this all Christmas too
Thank you Jesus for seeing us through.

*Cath Johnston*

### Consumer Boom Bang!

Munching McDonalds and gurgling coke.
She sits sharing one of yesterday's jokes.
Spend-thrift burns a hole in her pockets,
silently boiling like tiny rockets.

Window shopping in the afternoon,
credit card fever will strike soon.
Her eyes twinkle at the red shoe,
undecided she takes black, red and blue.

Oblivious to the falling rain,
unhindered her stamina will remain.
An armful of shopping is no chore
and the pleasant pain reprieves on sight of her door.

Moving inside she lays the bags down.
Opening each in turn with a chuckle and frown.
Clearing tins which click and clang.
She sighs after her consumer boom bang!

***J R Griffiths***

## THE JELLY ON THE PLATE

The jelly on the plate
is for my mate
who's sitting on the garden gate

Wibble, wobble, wo
it's going to and fro

It goes down your throat
just like a slug
it's like a whirlpool going
down your plug

The jelly was great
just like my mate
who is Kate.

*Hayley Mason*

## Past Times

In the still of the night,
you came holding the candle
with its flame,
throwing shadows in the
corners of my mind,
revealing all the memories
once again that were lost
in the ever running sands
of time in the still of the
night I see you the candle
and its light,
in the shadows of my mind
you lighten all the back roads
as I walk into past times.

*V N King*

## THE EYES

The eyes they are a most wonderful thing.
The love and lust that they can bring.
The things you can say with just a look.
You could even write a book.
About the words the eyes can say
Without ever making you say . . .
A sound.
They are always looking around
To see in what mischief they can get.
With just that look . . . where eyes have met
Across a room . . . across a table.
Distance does not seem able
To stop those eyes from passing the message
Whether through a window or along a passage.
The eyes they are a wonderful thing
With everything that they can bring!

**Colin Douglas Growns**

## TERRORS

Because we lived in a 'war time' industrial town,
We dreaded each night, of that air raid siren sound.
Shells were exploding, high in the air,
Buildings were burning, nearly everywhere.
Bombs would whistle, as they rained down.
Nerves were shattered, many lives lost,
For our town, this is what 'World War II' cost.
Now, another 'terror' has come back,
Because of the actions of local riff raff.
We fear walking, in our park,
Even a stroll, is a risk, in the dark.
Many muggers, burglars, and murderers, lurk,
While there are so many people, crying out for work.
That terrible war, many years ago, may have ceased,
What have we to do now, we fear our so called peace . . .

*Brian Marshall*

# SUBMISSIONS INVITED
*SOMETHING FOR EVERYONE*
**POETRY NOW '99** - Any subject, any style, any time.

**WOMENSWORDS '99** - Strictly women, have your say the female way!
**STRONGWORDS '99** - Warning! Age restriction, must be between 16-24, opinionated and have strong views.
(Not for the faint-hearted)
All poems no longer than 30 lines.
Always welcome! No fee!
Cash Prizes to be won!
Mark your envelope (eg *Poetry Now)* **'99**
Send to:
Forward Press Ltd
Remus House, Coltsfoot Drive
Woodston, Peterborough, PE2 9JX

**OVER £10,000 POETRY PRIZES TO BE WON!**

Judging will take place in October 1999